Hops & Bros Presents
CRAFT BEER 101

ALL ABOUT
HOPS

WRITTEN BY
CHRISTOPHE PAQUETTE
& MAXIM SAUMURE

ILLUSTRATED BY
DAVID BUIST

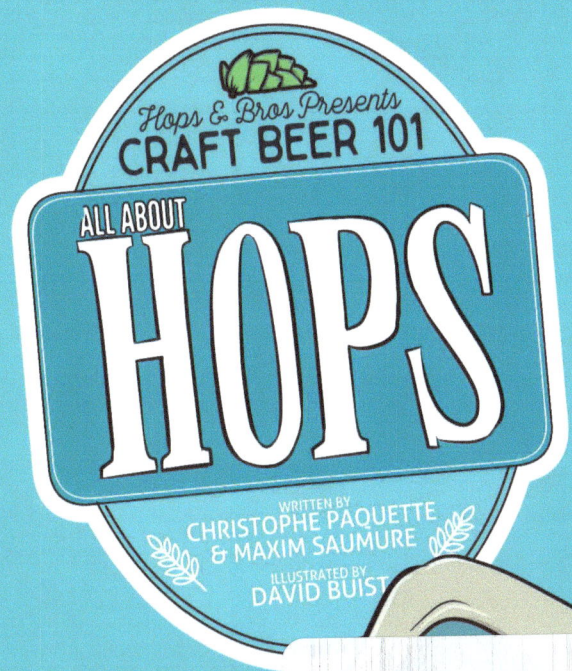

Printed in USA
First Printing, 2020

Editor: Amy Waeschle

ISBN: 978-1-7349272-2-1

Published by Zarfling Platoon
info@zarfling.com
zarfling.com

I0115153

HOPS

Don't let their soft flower exterior fool you. Hops may be delicate on the outside but they are most definitely bitter on the inside.

Bees won't be making honey with these plants. Instead of sweet pollen, hops have lupulin glands which produce a yellow powder that brewers covet.

When heated, the alpha acids in lupulin powder alters and help balance beer with a dose of bitterness.

The longer a hop is boiled, the more bitter is extracted, but these hops have another trick up their sleeve. The other essential oils present bring in a dose of citrus flavor. All a hop wants to be is grapefruit juice with a kick.

Lupulin powder is a key component nestled inside the hop. This glowing yellow sticky powder contains all the necessary acids to build the aroma and bitterness of beer.

Hops come in these forms: full cones, crushed, shredded, pellets, cryo, concentrate, and pure lupulin powder.

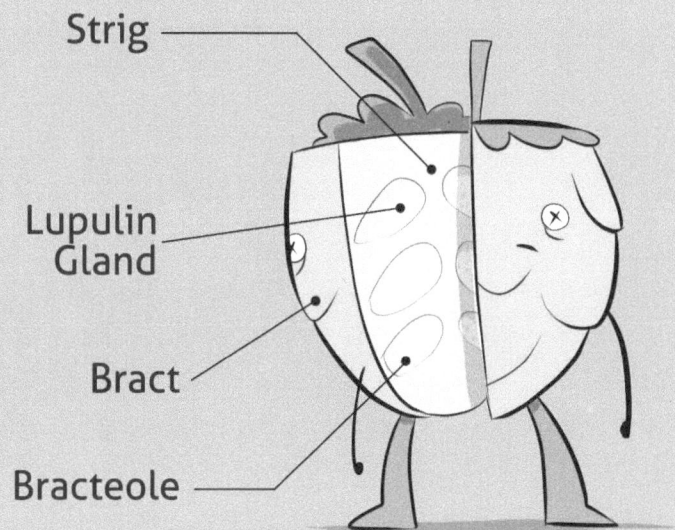

MAGNUM

This base bittering hop created in Germany in the 80's turned out to be one of the most popular variety grown in the US.

High acid alphas provide a clean-tasting bitterness with subtle citrus. One legend says that the Magnum hop grows better than Tom Selleck's mustache...

"Remember I told you I didn't like getting egg on my face? Well, right now, I'm wearing a whole omelet."

— Thomas Magnum (Tom Selleck)

Hop Facts

According to regular harvest periods and average yield from every year.

Alpha Acids	12-14%	**Purpose**		bittering
Beta Acids	4.5-5.5%	**Styles**		lagers & pale ales
Co-Humulone Composition	24-25%	**Country**		GERMANY & USA

WILLAMETTE

This massively important hop in the history of hops in America officially entered the market in 1971.

This pioneer grew up in Willamette Valley, Oregon, running around fields and wild rivers.

Willamette hops account for 20% of American hop harvest.

Complex spice aromas of floral and fruity tones converge with Willamette hops, making it a brewer's favorite.

Hop Facts

According to regular harvest periods and average yield from every year.

Alpha Acids	4-6%	Purpose		aroma
Beta Acids	3-4%	Styles		ales
Co-Humulone Composition	35%	Country		USA

AMARILLO™

Also known has VGXP01, Amarillo™ is a true citrus artist. Punchy and colorful, it shines with powerful tangerine aromas and a high acidic profile.

He won't hesitate to paint a pale ale like one of your French hops.

Hop Facts

According to regular harvest periods and average yield from every year.

Alpha Acids	8%	**Purpose**	aroma
Beta Acids	7%	**Styles**	pale ale
Co-Humulone Composition	8%	**Country**	USA

CENTENNIAL

The Centennial hop was created in the 1970s by Charles (Chuck) Zimmerman and S.T. Kenny, while working for U.S. Department of Agriculture at Washington State University.

The Centennial hop is versatile, helping to balance a beer with its citrus tones while adding depth.

Respect your elders.

Hop Facts
According to regular harvest periods and average yield from every year.

Alpha Acids	11.5%	Purpose		bittering & aroma
Beta Acids	4.5%	Styles		ESB, barley wine, IPA
Co-Humulone Composition	30%	Country		USA

IDAHO 7™

Special agent Idaho 7™ was dispatched with the code name 007 Golden Hop by a farm in Idaho back in 2015.

Strong and skilled with a level of high acid alphas. Sharp pine aromas, minty with some tones of oranges and tangerines.

Mr. Bond wishes his next bold IPA to be shaken, not stirred.

Hop Facts
According to regular harvest periods and average yield from every year.

Alpha Acids	13-15%	Purpose	bittering & aroma
Beta Acids	4-5%	Styles	IPA & pale ale
Co-Humulone Composition	30-40%	Country	USA

TOPAZ

This hop has quite an adventurous story that hails from the vast Australian countryside. By pursuing the perfect hop, Australian farmers ended up with this gem: Topaz.

Topaz's fruity aromas of lychee and clove spice tones shine bright in high gravity beers.

Hop Facts

According to regular harvest periods and average yield from every year.

Alpha Acids	17.7%	**Purpose**		bittering & aroma
Beta Acids	7-9%	**Styles**		IPA & pale ale
Co-Humulone Composition	51%	**Country**		Australia

EKUANOT®

Legend says that this hop performs better on the Equinox. Developed in the US back in 2014, it's been used in many different styles of beer.

Bright aromas of berries, lime, and melon boost the brightness of this hop.

Perfect for dry hopping (adding hops late in the brewing process to add more of the aroma), due to its high levels of myrcene and humulene.

Hop Facts

According to regular harvest periods and average yield from every year.

Alpha Acids	15.5%	**Purpose**	bittering & aroma
Beta Acids	5.5%	**Styles**	IPA & pale ale
Co-Humulone Composition	38%	**Country**	USA

GALAXY®

The mad scientist of the pact, Galaxy® quickly shone upon the brewing industry by sporting the highest content of essential oils of any hop variety.

Galaxy® is a trademark brand that for now is growing in Australia.

Intense in both citrus and grapefruit aromas, Galaxy® tends to mellow down over time in a finished beer.

Hop Facts
According to regular harvest periods and average yield from every year.

Alpha Acids	11-16%	Purpose		bittering & aroma
Beta Acids	5-7%	Styles		IPA & pale ale
Co-Humulone Composition	42%	Country		Australia

COLUMBUS

Deeply rooted in the Americas, Columbus was discovered in the Yakima valley. Built to suit a wide range of American style beer, maybe Christopher Columbus would have been even more well known if he discovered these hops instead..

This citrusy hop with herbal notes is flexible for use in both bittering and for aroma.

Hop Facts

According to regular harvest periods and average yield from every year.

Alpha Acids	14-18%	Purpose		bittering & aroma
Beta Acids	4.5-6%	Styles		brown ale, barley wine, stout
Co-Humulone Composition	28-35%	Country		USA

SAAZ

The noble queen has arrived! Saaz rules the helm of brewing in Europe and has been a dominant figure in the hops industry.

Saaz reigns over the most beloved pilsners of Czech Republic. High in acids, it creates floral and herbal aromas.

God save the queen!

Hop Facts
According to regular harvest periods and average yield from every year.

Alpha Acids		4.5%
Beta Acids		6%
Co-Humulone Composition		28%

Purpose	bittering & aroma
Styles	brown ale, barley wine, stout
Country	Czech Republic

SUMMIT

Nested on top of the highest mountains, this dwarf breed of hops was developed in the 2000's.

Complex and adventurous, it abounds in citrusy aromas like orange and grapefruit, and contains elevated amounts of acid alphas.

Hop Facts
According to regular harvest periods and average yield from every year.

Alpha Acids	18%	
Beta Acids	4.3%	
Co-Humulone Composition	33%	

Purpose	bittering
Styles	IPA, imperial stout
Country	USA

CHINOOK

Chinook dropped into the scene in 1985 just like Stallone's classic Rambo: First Blood Part II. This strong hop was keen to be part of the classic C hop family alongside Citra, Centennial, Columbus, and Cascade.

Aggressive in its pine character, you also taste hints of grapefruit tones. Many classic Strong Ales were developed featuring this hop.

"To survive a war, you gotta become a war. "
- John Rambo (Sylvester Stallone)

Hop Facts
According to regular harvest periods and average yield from every year.

Alpha Acids	14%	Purpose	bittering & aroma
Beta Acids	4%	Styles	IPA, stout, lager, porter, ale
Co-Humulone Composition	34%	Country	USA

ADMIRAL

England ruled with a strong navy and this admiral has seen many seas. Created as a high acid alpha in 1998 to replace Target hops.

Admiral is the perfect choice for classic British styles like ESBs and bitters. Used as a bittering hop, it anchors the brew with that balance of bite and grace.

Hop Facts

According to regular harvest periods and average yield from every year.

Alpha Acids	16.2%	Purpose	bittering
Beta Acids	6.1%	Styles	IPA, ESB, pale ale
Co-Humulone Composition	45%	Country	UK

SPALT

Known as one of the highest-ranked hops in the hop monarchy, Spalt is a classic variety that dates back to the 8th century.

Spalt hops were the first to receive the prestigious German Hop Seal. Its spicy character and earthy tones make it a first choice in classic German brewing styles.

Hop Facts
According to regular harvest periods and average yield from every year.

Alpha Acids	5.7%	Purpose	aroma
Beta Acids	5%	Styles	IPA, ESB, pale ale
Co-Humulone Composition	29%	Country	Germany

SIMCOE®

Don't be fooled by its strong punch. Characterized as a Cascade on steroids, Simcoe® plays nice with others.

Simcoe® popped on the brewing market in the 2000's, and became quite popular for its unique blend of aromas and piney punch.

Hop Facts

According to regular harvest periods and average yield from every year.

Alpha Acids	14%	Purpose	bittering & aroma
Beta Acids	5%	Styles	IPA, ESB, pale ale
Co-Humulone Composition	20%	Country	USA

VIC SECRET

Not related to lingerie company, Vic Secret was born in Victoria, Australia and valued for her sexy notes of tropical fruit and spice when used later in brewing.

Vic Secret provides mostly aroma in a beer but be reassured that she will spice things up with notes of passionfruit and pineapple.

Hop Facts

According to regular harvest periods and average yield from every year.

Alpha Acids	17%	Purpose	bittering & aroma
Beta Acids	7.8%	Styles	IPA, ESB, pale ale
Co-Humulone Composition	56%	Country	Australia

BROOKLYN

Completely unrelated to the famed Brooklyn rap trio Beastie Boys, Brooklyn is a variety developed in New Zealand. Due to lack of success, it's now performing under a new name: Moutere.

Moutere is a tasty addition to wheat beers and fruited hopped styles plus hits big flavor in big IPAs. Though it hasn't blown up like the other fruity varieties out there, Brooklyn offers hints of passionfruit, lime, grapefruit, and touches of hay.

Hop Facts
According to regular harvest periods and average yield from every year.

Alpha Acids	17.5-19.5%	**Purpose**	bittering & aroma
Beta Acids	8-10%	**Styles**	IPA
Co-Humulone Composition	26%	**Country**	New Zealand

CITRA®

01101000 01101111 01110000 01110011

Citra® stormed into the industry like AI is blowing up right now in our day-to-day lives.

Developed in a lab as X114, Citra® imposed itself as one of the first-ever citrus bombs. The high level of myrcene creates a unique blend of grapefruit, lime and tropical fruits.

Hop Facts
According to regular harvest periods and average yield from every year.

Alpha Acids	15%	Purpose	bittering & aroma
Beta Acids	4.5%	Styles	IPA, ales, amber
Co-Humulone Composition	35%	Country	USA

MOSAIC®

Love child of King Simcoe® and Queen Nugget, Mosaic® is much more powerful than Citra® and is even considered the boosted version of this hop.

Mosaic® is idolized for its triple-use capabilities (bittering, flavoring & aromas), is currently ruling the juicy IPAs kingdom with flying colors.

Hop Facts
According to regular harvest periods and average yield from every year.

Alpha Acids	13.5%	**Purpose**	bittering & aroma
Beta Acids	3.9%	**Styles**	IPA & pale ale
Co-Humulone Composition	26%	**Country**	USA

MANDARINA BAVARIA

Don't be confused, there's no tangerines growing in Germany. (Although, some experiment gone wild may have led to a weird crossover.)

In the wake of American juicy hop popularity, German hop growers bred Cascade, Hallertau Blanc & Hüll Melon to create a new juicy hop, perfect for dry hopping.

Hop Facts

According to regular harvest periods and average yield from every year.

Alpha Acids	10.5%	
Beta Acids	6.5%	
Co-Humulone Composition	33%	

Purpose	aroma
Styles	ale
Country	Germany

NELSON SAUVIN

Complex, complicated and subjective, Nelson Sauvin is a great addition to any party. This hop's actual punch and uniqueness make it a great conversation-starter (unlike your casual-wine-sipping sommelier friend).

Created in the early 2000's and named after its wine counterpart Sauvignon Blanc. This hop has been highly praised for its white wine and gooseberry aromas.

Hop Facts

According to regular harvest periods and average yield from every year.

Alpha Acids	13%	Purpose		bittering & aroma
Beta Acids	8%	Styles		IPA & pale ale
Co-Humulone Composition	24%	Country		New Zealand

EL DORADO®

From the deep jungles of the Yakima valley resides this impressive jewel: the Eldorado®. Adventurous brewers across the globe are still figuring out the mystery behind this shiny new nugget.

Launched in 2010, Eldorado® offers an impressive set of stats: great acid alphas, oils, yield and aromas of pear, stone fruit, and candy tones.

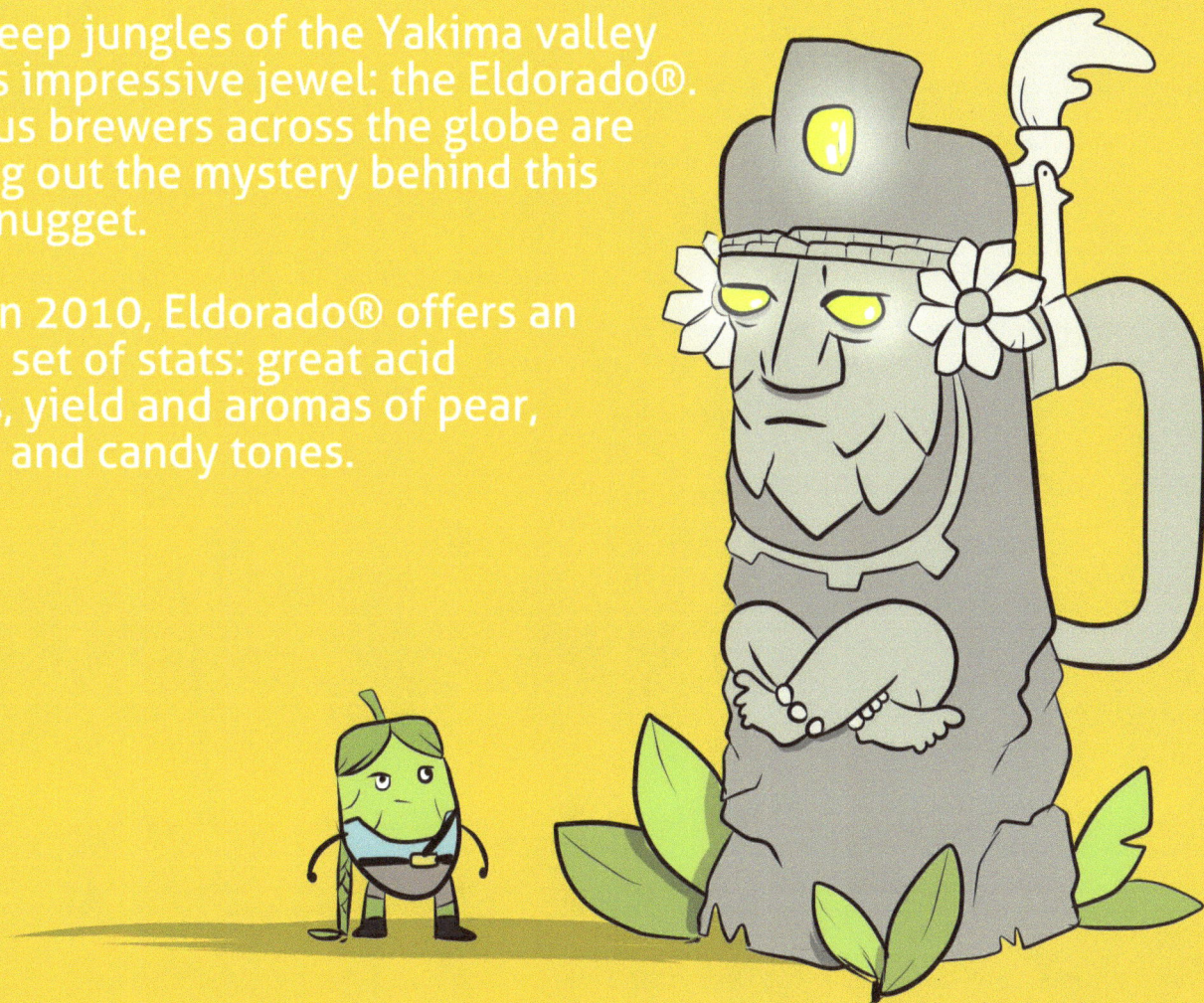

Hop Facts

According to regular harvest periods and average yield from every year.

Alpha Acids	13%	**Purpose**	bittering & aroma
Beta Acids	8%	**Styles**	IPA, wheat
Co-Humulone Composition	30%	**Country**	USA

CASCADE

The holy grail of the craft beer revolution, Cascade ignited the beer scene with its amazing, fresh aromas and characteristics that triggered the IPA craze.

Released in 1972, Cascade lead the craft beer revolution by being the crown jewel in what are now known as legendary hoppy IPAs and ales.

Hop Facts

According to regular harvest periods and average yield from every year.

Alpha Acids	4.5-8.9%	**Purpose**		bittering & aroma
Beta Acids	3.6-7.5%	**Styles**		IPA
Co-Humulone Composition	33-40%	**Country**		USA & Canada

LUMBERJACK™

From the deepest forests of the Great White North, this strong and pungent hop is a master of the woods, Hockey Night in Canada, and the fresh, cool breeze of the forest.

Trademarked by hop growers in British Columbia, this powerful hop offers fantastic alpha acids with a nice melon & spicy aroma, eh?

Hop Facts
According to regular harvest periods and average yield from every year.

Alpha Acids	10.1%	Purpose		aroma
Beta Acids	3.5%	Styles		ale
Co-Humulone Composition	28.1%	Country		Canada

AZACCA®

Working hard in the fields all day always calls for a beer, and Azacca®, who shares its name with the Haitian god of agriculture, would wholly approve.

Bred from a dwarf-hop-bittering program, it's not well as well known as it should be for its spicy notes and amazing mango aroma.

Raise an IPA to the farmers out there!

Hop Facts
According to regular harvest periods and average yield from every year.

Alpha Acids	14-16%	Purpose		bittering & aroma
Beta Acids	4-5.5%	Styles		IPA
Co-Humulone Composition	38-45%	Country		USA

WAI-ITI

Smooth, laid back, and joyful, Wai-iti, rewards the ones who wait with aromas of lime and stone fruit. Always make room in the cooler for a good catch like this one.

With a low content in both alpha and beta acids, this hop promotes a nicely rounded citrus tone and stone fruit aromas.

Hop Facts
According to regular harvest periods and average yield from every year.

		Purpose	aroma
Alpha Acids	2.5-3.5%	**Purpose**	aroma
Beta Acids	4.5-5.5%	**Styles**	IPA, pale ale, wheat beer
Co-Humulone Composition	22-24%	**Country**	New Zealand

SABRO

Celebrating the graduation class of 2018, Sabro (proclaimed rookie of the year) shook the industry with a truly unique aroma profile. Get ready for a coconut slam dunk in your favourite IPAs.

Developed over nearly two decades by the Hop Breeding Company, Sabro is built with the world's most popular aromas in mind. It contains strong notes of tangerine and coconut.

Hop Facts

According to regular harvest periods and average yield from every year.

Alpha Acids	12-16%	**Purpose**	aroma
Beta Acids	4-7%	**Styles**	IPA, pale ale, wheat beer
Co-Humulone Composition	20-24%	**Country**	USA

Yakima Valley in the US leads the way with innovative new hops like Mosaic ®, Citra ® and Sabro ®.

Europe has been the motherland of noble hops with Germany and Czech Republic producing most of the hops across the globe.

There's also a surge of new markets in other parts of the world like South Africa, Japan, Australia, and New Zealand.

WORLD OF HOPS

Hops have made beer special for so long that we tend to forget their origin stories, their background, or even the impact they have on our agricultural world.

Hops have a promising future. New strains are being developed each year, contributing to a diversity of beer flavors around the world. Eventually beer drinkers will be able to taste the nuances of terroir, like wine. Beer drinkers will be treated to exciting developments! If you are a hop grower out there, thanks for all the hard work! Cheers!

Hops & Bros has been put up together by two college friends, Max, a brewer & Chris, a marketing expert. Driven by their passion for video making and craft beer, they created a striving YouTube channel built around education and entertainment.

Scan with your smart phone to watch Hops & Bros

@HopsandBros

@david_buist

David Buist is a life long doodler, whose art style was created and developed in the margins of school notebooks and meeting notes.

"Looking for some fun, crafty visuals to engage with that utilize a clever blend of adult humor and that nostalgic, childhood feel of animated cartoons? Then look no further than @david_buist. Capturing the visual appeal of children's book illustrations, his work is the perfect concoction of playful yet witty."

- Floated Mag

www.ingramcontent.com/pod-product-compliance
Lightning Source LLC
Chambersburg PA
CBHW060845270326
41933CB00003B/200